HAUNTED BY WORDS LEFT UNSPOKEN

Release Regret,
A Buonomo

ANNA MARIE BUONOMO

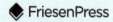 FriesenPress

One Printers Way
Altona, MB R0G 0B0
Canada

www.friesenpress.com

Artist: Joanne Bryant
Photo of author: Joseph Oliverio

ISBN
978-1-03-919448-9 (Hardcover)
978-1-03-919447-2 (Paperback)
978-1-03-919449-6 (eBook)

1. SELF-HELP, PERSONAL GROWTH, HAPPINESS

Distributed to the trade by The Ingram Book Company

www.annamariebuonomo.com
Instagram @annamariebuonomo

DEDICATION

To the people who have crossed my path—for
a reason, a season, or a lifetime—thank you
for being a part of my journey and helping me
become who I am today.

TABLE OF CONTENTS

AUTHOR'S NOTE

IN THIS BOOK, I use the terms "God" and "the universe" interchangeably. There may be other words that resonate with you, but in the case of these stories, know I am referring to a higher power.

INTRODUCTION—REGRET

REGRET GETS HEAVIER as we age. Time gives us an opportunity to look back on life and reflect on our actions or inactions. As far as I can remember, the words "time machine" seemed like the perfect solution to all problems. If only we could turn back the clock and undo or redo something we regretted, would that erase our pain? Would that save our souls? Still, to this day, many stories and movies with time machines and time travel give us a glimpse of what could happen. Unfortunately, the end warns us that it is best NOT to go back. Just as Newton's third law states, "For every action, there is an equal and opposite reaction." If we could go back into the past and change just one regret, there would be a domino effect that would follow and change the trajectory of our lives. Recognizing our regrets, and learning from them, has shaped us into who we are today. For some, that is wonderful; but for many, it is heartbreaking.

For those heartbroken from their past regrets, it is not too late to make peace with your past and heal your heart and soul.

According to research professor and author, Brené Brown, "Both disappointment and regret arise when an outcome was not what we wanted, counted on, or thought would happen."[1] In her research, it was found that what we regret most are our failures of courage. It is with this realization that we must find the courage to speak our truth and set our past free.

For those trying to seek forgiveness and make amends with the past, this book is for you. The calling to write this book comes from my desire to help others. At a very young age, all I wanted was to make a difference in people's lives, and it was for this reason that I became a teacher. As an educator, I am constantly learning how to support the people in front of me, providing them with the skills to find their version of success in life.

My call to help others has attracted the troubled, the heartbroken, and the seekers of change. I love to listen to people share their lives, and as I have gotten older, the stories have become more vulnerable and painful. Serving others is what brings purpose to my life.

The common theme within all these stories is regret: what people should have done or could have done, but did not. It is about living with mistakes that cannot be erased. Instead of dealing with their mistakes, many people set them aside as if they do not exist. Others hold them tight, and it is all they see and feel. Very few learn how to let go.

The purpose of this book is to shed light on the heavy topic of regret, specifically the regret of words left unspoken. The book is divided into three parts: the past, the present, and the future. Each section will address topics related to a soul's journey: trying to let go of the past, the challenges of living in the present, and how to create a promising future. The letters you will read written by Regret to the Past will provide insight into a tormented soul's journey of speaking their truth to set the past free. As you journey through this book, my hope is that you can replace the personified Past with your own subject of regret. The letters to the Present are about the struggles of living fully in the moment and how the past still lingers. At the end of Part II, the soul's journey finally faces the truth about how to truly make peace with the past to move forward. The future is unwritten, therefore, the letters from Regret do not continue. The section on the future provides strategies on how we can help our future selves today, to live a more fulfilled life.

Throughout the book, I will be sharing my personal experiences and providing advice to help you with your journey in speaking your truth to set your past free. May the letters, poetry, inspirational quotes, topics, and personal stories resonate within you and guide you to recognize that it is not too late to speak what has been hidden in your heart.

PART I:
THE PAST

HOLDING ON

IN THIS SECTION, you will read one soul's letters to a person they once loved from the past. All eleven letters begin with Dear Past as *Past* represents the person's name. The letters are signed by *Regret*, representing the person holding onto the regret. You will journey with the person known as *Regret* and experience the deep guilt and pain they have been holding onto for many years.

Following each letter, there is a poem that will express some of the unspoken words more profoundly. There are also topics that will address the theme in the letters. Within the topics, you will read about my personal experiences, along with guidance.

LETTER #1

Dear Past,

It's been a long time since we've seen each other. I hope you're doing okay. I'm not doing so well, and it's because of you. I've been doing a lot of thinking about my mistakes, and I feel stuck replaying moments that I can't undo or erase, and because of that, I'm struggling to fully experience the present.

At this point, I don't think I can move on. I keep hearing your voice telling me your fears, and in the end, I turned them into a reality. How could I do that to you? You saw me as your light, always there guiding you. I was your everything, and I turned my back on you. I see visions of you, and I'm haunted by our last goodbye.

As I slowly walk through life, I swear I've seen you from afar, but I know it couldn't be you as God parted our paths so long ago. It pains me to remember that we were once together, holding hands and laughing as one.

I must remind myself that you have brought me great joy, but at the same time, you have equally brought me great suffering. The good times fill my heart with so much love and laughter, and I want to hold those memories and feelings forever. I'm afraid I will forget you and that you will not remember me. I keep coming back to you because of the fear of never knowing you again. I try to relive all of you, which in turn brings me agony because I know how it ends. You must help me, Past, to put you behind me, to help me accept the things I can't change and keep your memories in the deep distance, to only visit you once in a while with the sense of peace and joy that you, at many times, brought me.

With deep sadness,

Regret

BROKEN

You were there,
And so was I.
Stuck in a moment
That would soon pass us by.
Not knowing what the future would hold,
Only haunted memories to be told.
Of words left unspoken,
Two hearts forever
Broken.

HAUNTED MEMORIES

*"In history as in human life, regret does not bring back
a lost moment and a thousand years will not recover
something lost in a single hour."* —Stefan Zweig

The past is a place that no longer exists, yet many people still live in their haunted memories. It is the people who once held a place in our hearts, and the people we once were, that make it difficult to move forward. If only we had dared to do things differently . . . would our present be more livable? Our past can no longer serve us, so we must let it go, but how? In the case of this soul, like so many souls out there, it is waiting patiently for its serendipitous encounter with someone from its past.

Why is it so hard to let go and move on? Why do we allow ourselves to suffer in this way? We are bombarded with positive messages about how LETTING GO will set you free, how it will make you feel better, and how it will help you move forward. Yet many of us choose to suffer in the present and, often, in silence. We lock our thoughts tightly away and put on a brave face to show the world that WE ARE OKAY! At what point do we admit that we are not?

Looking back on my life, I can see the regrets that broke me. Growing up, I was extremely shy and kept a lot of my thoughts to myself. My fears of speaking up filled my heart with many unspoken words. If only I had said this or that, the outcome would have been better and less painful. I guess that is why I turn to writing to express myself. It is only when I got older that I started to push myself to work on being more of an extrovert and speak what is on my mind.

What I learned is that we need to let ourselves feel regret and use our senses without judging ourselves. We need to allow the emotions to arise, then name those emotions and sit with them. We cannot push or ignore these feelings. We need to acknowledge them to put ourselves back together.

Imagine the past showing up today, and you came face-to-face with it; what would you say? Through a fortunate stroke of good luck, life does present these opportunities when we run into people from our past; they present themselves as a way to make amends, give us closure if needed, and help us find the courage to speak our truth. These synchronistic moments arise when we think of someone, and run into them, or they call or text us unexpectedly; this confirms that we are on the right track in life. But, what if those opportunities do not or cannot arise? This is when we need to speak or write out the words concealed in our hearts.

LETTER #2

Dear Past,

I was just starting to forget about you when a song on the radio made me think of you. It wasn't a sad song, but a happy one. The first verse struck my heart and triggered a memory of our younger years that I thought had been lost forever.

It brought me back to a time when I was happy with myself. I was living with the joy in my heart that I shared with you. Life was so simple back then, and it seemed as though it was just you and me. I could feel your hands holding mine, smell the fresh morning air from our walks under the old hanging trees, and hear your laughter echoing down the streets. I sat there thinking it was a sign from you to find you again. It left me with a temporary smile, but then it trickled deep into my soul, and sadness crept in. It feels like an indelible mark has been left on me because of you. I could hear your call for me to come back to you, but I must live in the moment and let you go. I keep telling myself I will. It has only been a few years; I can't imagine it will be forever. . .

Do you feel the same way I do? Or is it just me stuck in these moments from long ago?

With deep sadness,

FLASHBACK

As the music lyrics spill out
So do the emotions.
Flashback
To
You.
Intertwined memories
Playing in my mind like an olden-day movie
Only seeing and not hearing.
It is like seeing you for the first time
I seal the memories
To protect them from ever disappearing.

IGNORING THE PAST

*"Music replays the past memories, awakens
our forgotten worlds and make our minds
travel."* —Michael Bassey Johnson

Many people try to ignore the past by pretending it never existed, but as we know, it will show up time and time again until we acknowledge it. It will show up in many ways through our senses. Our powerful sense of smell, a familiar sound, a memorable taste, the touch of an object, or an unforgettable image can trigger a memory we have suppressed. Emotions—such as happiness, joy, anger, or sadness—arise, and they may remind us of our past regrets.

One sound that powerfully evokes our memories from the past is music. Music has the intense ability to bring the past back to the present instantaneously. We can almost feel the emotions of living in a time so long ago.

Music awakens emotions that we may have thought no longer existed in our souls. It makes us feel connected and gives us a sense of nostalgia. According to Shahram Heshmat, PhD, "Implicit memory is a form of classical conditioning. An event, an emotion, and a song get connected through implicit memory. When a piece of music is paired with a very emotional event, it can be an effective cue to bring back the strong emotion that was felt at that moment."[2]

Hearing a song can make us yearn to go back in time. Why do we want to go back? Most of the time, it is a joyful longing for moments that mean so much to us. But remembering a painful time can sometimes bring on deep sorrow. These mixed emotions are there to provide guidance and gratitude. We can be thankful for the good times and learn from the not-so-good times.

Music strikes my inner emotions on so many levels. I grew up with music constantly playing on our record player or radio. It was as though music understood me. I could feel at a young age the deep pain of a heartbreak song, the love that was meant to be, or the exhilaration of a new relationship. Even if I had no words to express myself, music always did, especially in difficult times, such as the teenage and young adult years. The powerful lyrics to a song helped to comfort me when I was feeling alone or heartbroken. Music seemed to have magical healing powers to help release emotions buried within.

Healing and overcoming adversity can both be supported by music. Music releases endorphins, which can lessen tension, anxiety, melancholy, and physical pain. Listening to upbeat music can improve our moods, as it raises the brain's serotonin levels. When we fail to describe our feelings, we might turn to music.[3]

The next time that song comes on the radio and takes you back in time, let it play out. Take the time to embrace it. Do not be haunted by it. Just welcome it, and accept it to move forward.

LETTER #3

Dear Past,

I need to snap back to reality . . . it's like a switch that keeps turning on and off. Most of the time I'm fully present, but like a switch, I return to a time and place I don't belong anymore. I have these conversations within my head as if they were real, as if they would transpire over a supernatural plane to the past.

Why am I having trouble letting you go? Clearly, we're not meant to see each other because if we were, it would have happened by now. I told you many moons ago that Destiny was pulling me away from you, and I said those famous words: "If it is meant to be, it will be, and God will cross our paths again." But when I said that, I truly believed deep in my heart that Destiny would be on my side and have our paths cross again. The hope in my heart was that we could see each other one last time to speak our unspoken words.

There is so much I want to say to you face-to-face; holding all these words in my heart is painful. I can't keep them locked up any longer. I'm afraid others will see what I have been hiding. I don't know what to do anymore. My faith must stay strong, and I must trust that the universe knows best. I must continue believing Destiny does not make mistakes, and this is the path I must stay on. My mind has to be stronger than my regretful heart.

With deep sadness,

Regret

DESTINED TO BE

I know it in my heart to be true
You and I are destined to be
Maybe not in this lifetime
Maybe in the next
I'll get it right
For in this lifetime
Destiny
Has other plans for me
That does not include you
My soul cries out in anguish
At the shock of the possibility
Of never seeing you again.

DESTINY

"It is not in the stars to hold our destiny but in ourselves." —William Shakespeare

There are numerous world views about destiny. Jewish traditions maintain that the Day of Judgment will take place following the coming of the Messiah. Jews hold the view that God determines a person's fate in the afterlife based on how good or bad they have been.[4] Christianity mentions destiny in the Bible as well. It teaches us that we were moral beings at the beginning of creation. We are responsible for choosing our destiny, but to fulfill our destiny, we must choose wisely.[5] The term *niyati* is used in Buddhism to describe the idea of fate or destiny. It refers to happenings that are predetermined, unavoidable, and unchangeable.[6] In Islam, although Allah is all-knowing, people still have choices. Obstacles will be put in your way, but how you deal with them is your decision. The human trial is one whose start and finish are predetermined.[7]

My grandmother, known as Nana, gave me many words of wisdom as I was growing up. I loved hearing her stories and sayings from her home country, Italy. She would first say them in Italian and then translate them for me into English. She always said that it never sounded quite right or as good as in Italian, but she always managed to help me comprehend the lesson or message. I remember her talking about destiny, saying, "Se deve essere lo sarà": if it is meant to be, it will be. I truly believed in those words. As simple as they were, they held power over me as a young girl trying to understand the meaning of life. Those words gave meaning to events that happened and events that did not.

As time passed and I grew older, I kept those words in my heart. Somewhere along the way, I started thinking I could make things meant to be. That, somehow, I could take control and make destiny work in my favour. For this to happen, I put a lot of focus on dreaming and visualizing what I wanted in my life, and I put my trust in God to help me along the way.

LETTER #4

Dear Past,

I am praying for a sign. A sign to let me know if what I am thinking and feeling is for real or if I am just wasting my thoughts away on you? I just need to know one thing: Are you thinking of me too? Are we still connected? Or am I crazy with these conversations in my head? Hoping that these thoughts will come to life in the real world. What will the sign need to be for me to believe it? It has to be a sign that can only come from your heart to mine, but what? The Universe speaks of many things. What did we once share that only you and I know? I am afraid it will come, and I will not recognize it, or I will doubt it. I must talk to God, and He will let me know.

Wish me luck; I can use it now. All I want is peace in my heart. Is that too much to ask?

With deep sadness,

Regret

A SIGN FROM YOU

A coincidence?
Not a chance!
A sign?
Confirm that!
I hear you Universe,
Calling out to see what's right in front of me.
Deep in my gut,
I know it to be true
A sign from you.
The repeating numbers.
The spirit animal flying over me.
The song lyrics of our favourite song playing out.
The mysterious dream
Showing me
What will soon become
A reality.

SIGNS

"When a person really desires something, all the universe conspires to help that person to realize his dream." —Paulo Coelho

What is the Universe telling us about our past? As humans, we are connected to everything. Is the Universe providing us with what we need instead of what we want? Sometimes, what we are looking for is right before us, but we cannot see it because we are always looking at what we left behind.

I am unsure where I learned to look for signs in the Universe, but I used it to confirm I was on the right track in life. It is quite fascinating how the Universe tries to communicate with us. If we try to stay in tune with our true selves, we can communicate more clearly with the universe and recognize the signs we are given. The most recognizable signs are synchronicities, dreams, numbers, animals or insects, recurring words, songs, and, most importantly, gut feelings. Gut feelings are the strongest signal from our intuition. Many times, we second-guess ourselves, which we regret later. This is where many of us need to improve.

I have always believed in signs and how the stars align with us. Maybe it was from all the romantic movies I watched over the years, or from asking and receiving, that I got the confirmation that what I was seeking was true. When my nana passed away, I was so upset with myself for not asking her on her deathbed: "What sign will you send me to know that you will still be with me?" This has been one of my biggest regrets because I was afraid and held back because death was quickly approaching.

Although I did not ask then, signs did appear. Her funeral was one of the most challenging days of my life. I wanted a sign so desperately; I wanted to know her soul still existed. It appeared in my daughter's purse: a little box lid with Nana's handwriting on it. I was shocked and could not understand how this had happened. It turned out my daughter had been playing with it on my mom's birthday two months prior, and she had forgotten to take it out of her purse. Seeing her penmanship in Italian filled my heart with serenity on such a sorrowful day.

In the book, *Signs: The Secret Language of the Universe*, psychic medium Laura Lynne Jackson proposes a method to seek signs from the otherside. One day on a walk with my dog, I felt so in tune with the universe that I decided to try her technique. I spoke to my nana and asked her to send me a dragonfly as a sign to confirm that she was still with me. At the time, it was winter, and I knew the sign would not be a real dragonfly. Days later, the signs started showing up in the strangest ways, and in the most unusual places. I saw dragonflies on television, received a stone carving of a dragonfly as a gift from my friend's travels, noticed them in a painting at the doctor's office, and even spotted earrings shaped like them in a store . . . the list goes on. In my heart, I knew this was not just a coincidence; this was the sign I had asked for and received, repeatedly, and I am so incredibly grateful.

Many people are not actively looking for signs, but they do show up, and it is only if we are alert that we can catch them. If we miss them, they will show up repeatedly until they are loud enough to get our attention. My all-time favourite book, *The Alchemist* by Paulo Coelho, has inspired many people to seek their calling in life. It is the story of a shepherd boy, Santiago, and his journey to realizing that his destiny contains a powerful message about following the signs (omens) that God has sent out from the universe to us. Each of us has the potential to find our purpose in life by listening to our hearts and learning to read the signs.

LETTER #5

Dear Past,

I've waited too long to seek help. Not even the healers can heal this broken heart of mine. I have searched for many people to help me heal from my brokenness, and the guilt that lives deep into my soul, but the grace I feel is only short-lived. It's not as though I haven't tried and prayed and repeated those steps. I've been told that the chains around my heart are unlocked. I'm fully aware now that I've been carrying them and that those chains have been weighing me down. It's hard to hear those words. All that is left on my heart are scars from you. Luckily, the world cannot see them.

So much time has passed, and I still feel the same. Everything feels temporarily hopeful; then time sinks in, and so does the pain. I suppose the saying "time heals all wounds" isn't true. Instead, time has only given me more opportunities to reflect and survive this pain.

I have to invite Jesus in to heal my heart. He knows my soul all too well. I just need to provide him with the space, and I just need to silence my mind to hear him.

With deep sadness,

FEAR

Fear still exists

Fear of what you would say back to me

Fear of you judging me

Fear of your disappointment

Fear to see your heart

Fear I will not be able to say goodbye one last time.

HEALERS

"The soul always knows what to do to heal itself.
The challenge is to silence the mind." —Caroline Myss

Healers come in many forms. Friends, family, doctors, religion, nature, and spirituality are just a few examples. Instead of turning inward, many people turn toward others and objects to heal themselves from great suffering. When it is agony from within, how can we heal it or fix it? No scan will show this invisible pain. The only one who can diagnose it is yourself.

When I think of the word "healer," my mind goes directly to Jesus. As a child raised in the Catholic faith, I was awestruck by the stories of Jesus from the Bible. He was not only a great teacher, but a healer. Many Christians today still believe that Jesus can heal us because he lives inside us. Whenever I got sick growing up, my mother would say, "If Jesus can heal, so can we, as Jesus is God, and he lives within us." She taught me that this is not just physical healing, but spiritual, emotional, and mental. My belief in God provided me with much guidance and solace.

Many Catholics visit an ordained priest to confess their sins. In the Sacrament of Reconciliation, people feel a weight has been lifted off their shoulders. The speaking of their sins and clearing of their guilty mind have brought many believers a sense of internal peace. At the end of their session, they listen attentively to the words of absolution and walk away, giving God thanks for the opportunity to begin anew.

My husband struggled with regrets. He loves to tell the story of how he finally went to confession after twenty-five years of holding in the guilt of his younger days. He lived decades with guilt and regret eating away at him, and all it took was for him to enter confession and speak his truth to be set free. It was his most healing experience. He could not go back in time and change his mistakes, but what he could do was speak and be forgiven. This worked for him, but for those with a different set of beliefs, you can still speak your truth by talking to a counsellor, a psychologist, a trusted friend, or a family member. You can even write a letter and burn it to release your unspoken words to the Universe. By doing so, you can get the necessary closure to help you move forward.

Healing ourselves is a whole body and mind process. Everything must come together for it to be successful. As we know, the mind is immensely powerful, and often, we may hear or use the phrase, "mind over matter." I believe this to be true; we have the willpower to overcome almost anything. It takes time, practice, and patience. You must be dedicated to putting the work in.

There are various ways to help with spiritual healing, such as chakra healing, Reiki, aromatherapy, energy healing, meditation, and visualization techniques, just to name a few. As for psychological healing, it is best to seek therapy to help change your state of mind. Take the time to seek support and find ways to do this work at your own pace.

It is important to remember that the healing process will have its difficulties. Just when we think the healing is done, a relapse can happen because suffering runs deep, and many things can trigger the pain to arise again. But with the right skills, people can learn to carry on with their lives and restore balance and harmony.

LETTER #6

Dear Past,

You appeared to me in a dream last night. It felt so real. I've dreamt about you many times, but I heard you speak last night. I've tried hearing you before, but you finally came through crystal clear.

I travelled afar with many others to find you. When we arrived at our destination, you weren't there, so we decided to wait. When you finally appeared, you were surprised to see me standing there. You held your pointer finger out—as if to tell me "No . . . it can't be you; you can't do this"; and you sat down. I walked a little closer, waiting patiently for you to talk to me, and when you did, you grabbed my hands tight. You declared, "Now that you are here, you can't go!" I tried to explain it all to you, and we sat for quite some time, and the others that travelled with me kindly waited. Knowing they were there, I quickly tried to get out all my unspoken words. I didn't want the dream to end; I tried to replay it while I was still dreaming, but it was too late; you were already gone.

When I woke up this morning, my heart was filled with hope that there could be a chance to see you again and finally say all the words I left unspoken.

With deep sadness,

Regret

IN MY DREAMS

Repeating the same unconscious desire
Suppressed thoughts
Show up every night
Reflection of what my soul truly seeks
Will this dream ever come to life?
Only time will tell.

DREAMS

"A dream not interpreted is like a letter which is not read" —The Talmud

Dreams come to us with messages to decipher and clues to uncover about ourselves, and if we dig deep enough, the answers will come to light. For as long as I can remember, dreams have meant something to me. My childhood friend and I would spend hours analyzing each other's dreams, even to this day. No book can truly give you the meaning of your dreams, but someone who knows you can.

Alan Eiser, a psychologist and clinical lecturer at the University of Michigan Medical School in Ann Arbor, says dreams can be "highly meaningful" because they "deal with the sort of personal conflicts and emotional struggles that people are experiencing in their daily lives."[8] Taking the time to journal your dreams can help you find patterns—even solutions—in your everyday problems.

Dreams can provide you with great insight into your psyche. Although there are common themes that many people share when they dream, your dreams are unique and highly personal. The things we experience in our dreams most likely reflect the concerns and/or excitement in our daily lives. Once you write down your dreams in detail, analyze the content as if it were a story and consider what it might mean in your daily life. Use your senses to uncover the true meaning behind your dreams.

In Dr. Alishia M. Alibhai's course *Exploring Past Lives: A Journey into Hidden Realms of the Soul*, dreams are a powerful gateway to our past lives. She believes that some of our dreams are actual memories from the past, especially those that feel real but do not quite make sense. Dreams can reveal a wealth of information about our former lives. Things that occur in our dreams can be from a past life.[9]

After my nana's passing, I had many dreams of her and longed to see and feel her presence again. Thanks to dreams, I have been able to do so. There was one dream I remember distinctly because it felt so real; it was as though I had been transported to another time and space. I was in my nana's old bedroom, where we lived during my childhood. I was fully aware that she had passed away. I opened the drawers to find something I could take of hers as a reminder. But unfortunately, the drawers were almost empty and contained only sheets and pajamas. I decided to open her top drawer and again was disappointed to find only pins and objects that held no significance. I felt deep grief as I could not find what I was looking for. Just as in my waking life, I was searching for something of my nana's to hold onto to fill the void of her absence.

Whatever you believe about dreams, know there may be something more profound for you to unveil to help you better understand your life. Take the time to dig deep. You might be surprised by what you may find.

LETTER #7

Dear Past,

I want peace—peace of mind, heart, and soul. I've carefully put out my intention with words that only put forth love. In a world so broken and full of fear, I want to create a world around me full of mercy and joy. I can feel it coming.

I believe that I can set my intentions, and they will manifest. I have this urgency in my heart to see you one last time. I don't want to carry this with me into my next life. The need to make peace must happen! It is my intention to stand in front of you and apologize for the hurt I may have caused you. It is that simple! All I want in return is to miraculously feel peace within.

With deep sadness,

SEED OF HOPE

To heal this wound
Is to put out the intention
That my heart will speak to yours.
I begin to plant the seed of hope as I begin a new day.
I set it to then release it.
I trust the universe will take care of the rest.

INTENTIONS

"Energy flows where my intention goes." —Gabrielle Bernstein

According to Gary Zukav, an intention is the level of awareness you bring to a word or deed. It is power. You are speaking for this reason. Your motivation determines the results.[10]

Whatever your intention is, set it with a positive mindset. As many of us believe, what you put out into the world is what you will get back. People use intentions when they want to manifest something significant in their lives. Manifestation is taking our thoughts and turning them into reality.

When setting an intention to manifest, follow manifestation coach Kenneth Wong's three key steps:

1. **Write your intention down**. Once your desire is on paper, proceed to elaborate and provide more information. Write down your plan of action and describe it with all five senses. Visualizing your desire in this step will assist you in setting your intention.

2. **Clarify the intention behind your desire.** Ask yourself why you want to manifest this desire. Record your response to this question and be truthful. You can only access the energy supporting your desire in this manner. For example, you attract people, circumstances, and experiences that reinforce your positive energy when you radiate high vibrational, positive energy. The same goes

for when you attract people, circumstances, and experiences that reinforce your bad energy when you release low-frequency, negative energy. Before moving to the next step, utilize manifestation strategies such as affirmations for alignment and prayers to the universe if you discover that your desire is supported by low vibrations.

3. **Declare your intention to the universe.** Read it out for the universe to hear it. Let go of the how, what, and when, and just let your good intentions uplift your soul.[11]

An example of an intention would be wanting to cross paths with someone from your past to make amends. Based on the above steps, this is what you can do:

Step 1. Write down your goal of wanting to run into that specific person. Visualize the encounter. Where would this take place? What words would be exchanged? Hear their voice speak to you. Feel the touch of the hug you may embrace. Take a deep breath in and smell the air surrounding the two of you. Look into their eyes and see the depths of their soul. Lastly, use your sense of taste to encompass the full sensory experience.

Step 2. Ask yourself why you want to run into this person. You have to be honest with yourself. Ensure that the energy you put out about this intention is positive. If your intention is backed by positive energy like happiness, peace, forgiveness and appreciation, you will attract more positive outcomes. Use affirmations such as: I'm open to seeing this person again or I have so much to say to this person.

Step 3. Confidently read your intention out for the universe to hear. This final step is releasing your desire to the universe and trusting that it has been heard and will be delivered when the time is right.

As simple as this process may seem, you must follow these steps correctly and practice them to change your thoughts and habits. Finally, you MUST surrender! You need to surrender your desire, NOT your intention. It is essential for you to truly believe in order to receive.

I know this process works. I did not know the process when I was younger, but I somehow visualized the life I wanted, and up until now, I got so much out of life. Deep within my soul, I recognized what was meant to come into my life. It is not to say I did not have many challenges and obstacles along the way; it is just that I had to put faith in what was best for my higher self. Putting your trust in a higher power lets you release control of what is to come.

Fortunately, there have been many remarkable stories of manifestation in my life, from meeting my favourite boy band group, finding my dream job, and marrying my soulmate to having two loving girls and so much more. Then there was the other side, when it did not always work out as I had planned, hoped, or wished for, but I kept my faith, knowing better things would come my way.

Just remember, we cannot force things to happen. We have to let go of what our ego thinks is best for us and trust that the universe will provide us with what is best for our higher selves. We need to trust the process and be patient for what is meant to be.

LETTER #8

Dear Past,

Another year has passed, and nothing. I thought I saw the signs. I believed that something phenomenal would come and we would run into each other. I have prayed, waited, and continued to believe, and here I am with emptiness and disappointment. How could I be so wrong? I felt so in tune with the Universe. Maybe the reality is that I'm left to suffer. I need to surrender to the idea that this is my ultimate punishment—a lifetime of torment, repeating the many versions of saying I am sorry with thousands of different scenarios playing out in my head like something out of a movie. It is heartbreaking to realize that I don't have the magical powers to reveal my deepest desire to make peace with you.

It looks like I am coming to the end. May you know deep within your heart how sorry I am to have hurt and betrayed you. I can only pray that you have found serenity in your heart for me. My wish for you is that you are truly riding out your best life.

With deep sadness,

Regret

UNRECOGNIZABLE

Mend this heart.
For it is broken into a million little pieces
Shattered
Scattered
Unrecognizable
Please rid me of this guilt and regret.

HOW DEEP IS THE PAIN?

*"Behind every beautiful thing, there's
some kind of pain."* —Bob Dylan

The most tremendous pain is the loss of a loved one. It is the forever goodbye that lingers on. It is the replaying of memories that soon starts to fade away. It is knowing that the pain may live on forever.

When we cut our ties with those who no longer serve us, we should feel a sense of relief. It is difficult to walk away or give up on those we once loved. The loss is not just for the person we departed from, but also for ourselves and the version of us that will no longer exist.

When the ties are cut without our approval, only time can see us through the reason as we reflect on life as we age. Sometimes what we want is not always the best for our future selves. Circumstances happen, and other people enter our lives to take us down a path that will serve us for the better.

When things do not go our way, we may blame others and our higher power. Especially when the loss was out of our control, and we did not plan for it or want it to happen. When my best friend lost her son to cancer at a youthful age, it shocked us all. We all gathered to pray for him to be healed and cancer-free. We genuinely believed that God heard our prayers for this nine-year-old to live a full life. The loss of this innocent and magnetic boy shook our souls. How could this happen? Why did this have to happen? This pain will forever be etched in our souls. There is no recovery from this ache. It will live within us forever, just as our love for him will.

Although the pain is deep within us, we have control over how much of it we allow to rise to the surface. We need to face our pain and tame it. We cannot hide from it or pretend it does not exist. We must show it, that way over time the pain will no longer control us. Just remember you are not alone, and you must seek support to help you get through it.

LETTER #9

Dear Past,

I know I betrayed you. The fear of telling you the truth got the best of me. We had such a trusting relationship, and the thought of a future together brought fear of the unknown. This voice told me it wasn't in the stars for us, and it was time to walk away. Since then, I have been committed to showing mercy to others in the hope that one day you will show me mercy too.

With deep sadness,

THE POWER OF MERCY

The power of mercy is held in your hands.
I wait patiently for the time to arrive.
To stand in front of you,
And hear you speak directly into my heart,
I forgive
I understand
I accept
All that you have done.
May this mercy set you free.

MERCY

"O God, be merciful to me, a sinner." —Luke 18:13

In a world that has so much darkness, this is when we need to show more mercy. Through acts of kindness, mercy can shed light on a time when we feel so lonely. Instead of seeking a grudge or planning an act of revenge, do the exact opposite—show mercy, and forgive. By doing so, hope sets in. By giving others a second chance, we also do this for ourselves. There will be a time when we will need it in return.

It will not be easy, and showing mercy may feel impossible, but only you can control how you react and want to live. Here are some simple ways to show mercy to others:

- Be kind, even toward others who may not be kind to you.
- Be patient with others who may not be who you want them to be, and accept them as they are.
- Help those in need, especially those who are hurting and have no one to turn to.
- Pray and speak your truth.
- Forgive not only others but yourself.

God has presented me with a great deal of opportunities to show mercy to others. They arrived when I was ready to see the truth and when there was room in my heart to forgive.

I have heard numerous stories of mercy. It is astounding if you think about it. Just when you think it is over and the bad blood will never disappear, in time, it can. The most common story I hear about is betrayal. It is the same heartbreaking tale of someone who breaks the trust of another. That deep hurt is hard to get over, but it is possible. When you are young and naive, it may take longer to heal from such experiences, potentially impacting your future relationships if not properly addressed.

It takes strength and courage to show compassion and forgive someone who deceived you. Many people want to hurt others back, but that does not heal them; it will only make the pain grow deeper and darker. Showing mercy and allowing those who have hurt you to come forth and speak their truth can also lead to healing, reconciliation, and a sense of closure. Find it in your heart to show mercy, and pray for those who may have caused you pain. They may have acted without understanding or were struggling to confront their own truths.

If I did not show mercy to my husband, who was not my husband at the time, we would not be married today. In our younger years, when we met, the timing was not right. As much as I thought he was the one, things were not in our favour. I realized that I could not make him happy, and it was up to him to find happiness within himself. It was difficult for me to do, and we parted ways. Years later, he appeared in my life again. This time, he was in a good place and was living a more fulfilled life. He wanted a second chance. After careful consideration, and following my heart, I showed mercy. That mercy brought me so much love, as I knew he was the one I was destined to be with, and I have been blessed with our beautiful family.

LETTER #10

Dear Past,

Looking back on my letter of intention, I see I got it all wrong. My desire to see you again in this life got in the way of my manifestation because of the urgency to control and worry about it coming to life. My fear of never seeing you again has clouded my mind and taken control of my every thought. The timeline that I put myself on, and the desire for it to manifest NOW, has caused the block. Letting go of these fears is challenging, and I'm losing control and unsure how to get back on track. I can't seem to truly surrender to the Universe and believe it has a better plan than I do. I need to find the strength and surrender, but how?

With deep sadness,

Regret

SET ME FREE

My hands are up
My knees are down
My heart is wide open
For all to see
Set me free!

SURRENDER

"Surrender to what is. Let go of what was. Have faith in what will be." —Sonia Ricotti

Surrendering seems like giving up, but it is not. It is finally realizing that you cannot change what was in the past and that it is time to let it go. Our thoughts of the past are holding us back from the future we all deserve. We must surrender and allow divine intervention to take over and lead. By surrendering, the possibility that something better will come opens up.

Gabrielle Bernstein, the author of *The Universe Has Your Back,* proposed the following actions to embrace surrender:

1. Release control through prayer.
2. Turn over time by accepting the present moment as a miracle.
3. Let faith guide you by letting go of your goals.
4. Release your desire to a higher power and trust it is being taken care of.[12]

When things did not work out for my husband and me in our early twenties, I had to surrender and hand it over to God. It came back to my belief in destiny—if it is meant to be, it will be. I had to let go. The years apart gave us time to grow and experience more out of life. I was not sad or angry anymore, and I lived that time with some adventure that I otherwise would not have experienced had I been with him. Those years meant something to me and changed me for the better. That is one decision I do not regret. By surrendering to the Universe, I was open to receiving something better, which eventually brought me back to him.

LETTER #11

Dear Past,

This is the end. My final letter to you. This must be my sign to release you. The Universe has shut down my wish and has other plans for me that don't include you. I have to let go of what my soul desires to seek since the peace it has been pursuing has only caused suffering. Isn't that ironic?

It is with the deepest regret that I did not have the courage or the opportunity to say these simple words to you: "I am sorry." I am sorry for turning my back on you. You were the one person that I trusted, and I betrayed you. I have not forgiven myself for that very reason. Maybe my hanging onto this is selfish because it is about my guilt and wanting to clear it. I wanted to apologize and let you know that I have only wished the best for you. And I wanted to know that you have no ill feelings toward me. I have prayed for strength and hoped that divine intervention would cause us to cross paths again. I have come to accept this is my reality.

Since the past was not a place for me, may the present bring me some joy. May I learn the lesson to go with my gut and trust my instincts because when I don't, I'm left with regret that could last a lifetime.

There will still be some deep hope that the stars align for us one day. I would like to thank the Universe for making our paths cross many moons ago.

With deep sadness,

Regret

NEW DAY

Wake Up!
Open your eyes to a new day.
Look around.
Count your blessings.
Feel the love.
Cherish the memories.
Let go of the pain.
Set yourself free today!

ACCEPTANCE

"The first step toward change is awareness. The second step is acceptance." —Nathaniel Branden

There comes a time in our lives, or numerous times, when we need to come to acceptance. The reality is that whatever our situation was is done, and we should not attempt to change it or go against it. By accepting, we can move forward and create a new reality. This one simple step can make all the difference. We can end our suffering if we take a chance on ourselves and change our thoughts about a situation.

The virtue of acceptance allows us to come to terms with our mistakes and learn from them. The serenity prayer states it best: "Lord, grant me the serenity to accept the things I cannot change, the courage to change the things I can, and the wisdom to know the difference." The time when I had to accept that my new reality would not include my husband, who at the time was my boyfriend, was difficult. It was not an easy decision or realization, but I knew I had to end my suffering, and I deserved much better. I accepted the fact that I could not change him, I found the courage to change my situation by ending the relationship with him, and I gained the wisdom to know that I needed to make a positive change in my life. It is important to realize our worth as an individual and that we do not need validation from another person. To live a life we love, we have to face truths that will be hurtful, but not as painful as if we were to live with lies and regrets.

To finally be free from the past, we have to face that at the end of the day, "It is what it is." That is acceptance! It is all that is left. No more fighting, resisting, or crying about how we wished things could be different. You can be free from the guilt of regrets.

BONUS LETTER: LETTER FROM THE PAST

If the past could respond to you, what words would you wish to hear to heal you? In the case of this soul's journey, these are the words that would help heal.

Dear Regret,

I heard your cries. I heard you call my name. I heard you in the darkest hours of the night. I spoke back to you. I forgive you. You will be forever imprinted in my soul, but only I know it is there. I have tried to forget and replace you more than once, but what is done is done and cannot be undone. The past is already written, and we can't change it, but you can change your present and your future. Stop wasting your time on me, as I am your history. It is time to move on and set me free. You have your entire future ahead of you, and the only way for it to be successful is for you to keep moving forward.

With the deepest love,

PART II:
THE PRESENT

TRYING TO MOVE ON

IN THIS SECTION, you will continue to read letters from Regret. The letters are addressed to *Dear Present,* representing the person whose name Regret has moved on with. You will continue to journey with *Regret* and experience how challenging it is for someone to move on and try to fully live in the present moment when their past is still lingering in their heart and mind.

Following each letter will be a poem that further expresses words that have been left unspoken to Past. There will be topics addressing the theme and struggles in each letter. Since this is focused on the present time, you will read about topics that people struggle with in their daily lives, along with advice to help you move on.

LETTER #13

Dear Present,

You should be happy that I am here with you. Well, at least that is what I keep telling myself. The truth is Past is still lingering with me, and I don't know how to get rid of them. I have already told Past that I'm moving forward and uttered, "I'm letting you go." But deep down, I'm still keeping Past alive. Present, I need you to help me be with just you!

Something is not sitting right with me. It is how I ended things with Past that haunts me today. I have always taken pride in being good and honest, but with Past, the fear of telling the truth made me ashamed. I'm trying to shield you from Past. They wanted forever, as did you, and I had to choose.

It was choosing to let go of Past with such haste that keeps me praying to be forgiven at night.

With love,

Regret

TRAPPED

In my memory's eye,
I see you so clearly
As if it were the
Present.
Your eyes smiling back at me.
It's who you were then
That traps me
Today.

LIVING IN THE PRESENT

"Whatever the present moment contains,
accept it as if you had chosen it. Always work
with it, not against it." —Eckhart Tolle

Here we are stuck between the past and the future. This period of existing is the NOW. For those trapped in the past, getting to the present will be challenging and living in it even more so. We live in a world full of distractions, and along comes stress, anxiety, and regret. We must navigate it all to get the most out of this life.

To fully live in the present, we must focus on the current moment by being more mindful of what is happening around us. Take the time to observe and notice the little things that make you happy, and give thanks. Do not worry about yesterday or tomorrow; just stay focused on your current day and smile, knowing that the day is another gift to be cherished. There are many unfortunate circumstances that people face, and many who are close to us do not get to see tomorrow. So, why dwell on the past or think of the future? They are both irrelevant to what you are doing today.

Letting go of someone you once loved, and moving forward with a new person, is healthy. First, it will take time to accept that the one from your past is gone and that you are blessed with a chance to start anew. That is why it is important to focus on living in the present, so you can create new memories to help you carry on. Live your life by being conscious and appreciating every gift that comes with each breath you take. Make that change. You can do it!

LETTER #14

Dear Present,

What is it going to take for me to escape Past? Today was challenging as I started to feel your presence, but that lasted only a short time. I had a relapse and started to worry about Past. What is Past doing? Are they stuck because of me? Did my role in Past's life cause harm? Will I ever find the answers to these questions controlling my thoughts and interfering with you? I really should not be caring about these things. I'm genuinely sorry. I truly am trying my best.

With love,

Regret

PANIC ATTACK

In the depths of my soul,
I hear you calling out for me
Pulling me in
Holding me tight;
Panic sets in
Knowing it's not right.

WHAT WILL IT TAKE
TO ESCAPE REGRET?

*"The attempt to escape from pain, is what
creates more pain."* —Dr. Gabor Maté

Have you ever held on so tightly to regret that you cannot
move forward? It is like an insidious force within you, and
over time it is spreading, more pervasive, and complex. What
will it take to break free from this overpowering regret?

Living in the present is tricky. You are fully aware of what
is happening, but you are still noticing quick moments of the
past move through your memory bank. Sometimes you let
these moments pass by as quickly as they came in. But other
times, you grab hold and cannot let go, and you are back at
square one AGAIN!

It is natural to think back on the past. It is a part of who
we are. The problem arises when we get stuck, especially
when we are trying to move on. Starting a new relationship
may bring up some unwanted feelings from a past loved one,
but as humans, we must understand that we cannot run
away from the past and the people that we once loved.

The new relationship you are developing in the present
has to be with someone who will not judge your past relationships. It is our past relationships that have helped shape
us and hopefully contributed to loving and learning.

We must take a different perspective on how pain can make us stronger and wiser if we learn from it, instead of dwelling on it. According to author and poet Yung Pueblo, "If the pain was deep, you will have to let it go many times."[13] And that is what happens to a lot of us. The deep pain of regret is a part of life. We cannot escape it. It is through facing our pain and overcoming it that the healing begins.

LETTER #15

Dear Present,

You have given me the greatest gift, and I thank God every day for you. But something is battling inside me, and I fear it will take me away from you. I feel like a fraud, trying to be that bright light when the light is already out inside. It's exhausting living like this. I wish I could let my guard down and show the world the truth behind the smiles. I want to tell you what I am thinking about, but I know how you feel about Past; therefore, I must keep my thoughts tightly locked forever. It is just that what I did to get here hurt Past. It was down to you or Past, and I chose you and would do it again in a heartbeat.

There is this constant urge to reach out to Past and apologize, but I know I should not because, in the end, it will only hurt you. So, my hurt must be buried and never come up again.

I will continue to stay true to what I know is best and not be led into temptation.

With love,

BATTLE WITH THE DEVIL

I blanket myself with smiles
Hoping nobody will notice my misery
I battle with the devil to not show its face to the world
I pull tighter, not to let it break free.

THE DEVIL IN DISGUISE

"The Devil tempts you to destroy your faith, God tests you to develop your faith." —Warren Wiersbe

It is terrifying how the devil shows up at your weakest moments and tries to convince you that he is your saviour. He makes you believe that giving into temptation leads you to peace. In those vulnerable moments, you try to tell yourself that God is leading you, but that voice stops you from following Him. You must keep telling yourself that you are stronger than the devil and will NOT give in, especially after all these years. Why start to be fooled by him now?

When we feel extremely helpless and prone to backing down, whether in small or significant things, we should understand that the devil is only tempting us because we are higher in dignity than he is. The devil only displays his resentment and envy by enticing us. When we oppose him or ask for forgiveness, we demonstrate the tremendous goodness we already possess.[14]

Deep down, you know what is best for you. If there is some underlying guilt that is encompassing your every thought, and is leading you to go against your morals, seek help. Do not let your guilt lead you astray! This would be a suitable time to write out the words you have been holding in. If you are in a trusting relationship and you feel comfortable sharing what has been holding you back from really embracing change, then open up. Writing or speaking your truth can put you on a path to redemption.

LETTER #16

Dear Present,

It is by living in the moment that I truly recognize the truth about myself: what I have done and what I have failed to do. It is finally admitting the truth for the first time, that what I had done was lie when I knew better, but still did it. What I failed to do was be honest and tell the truth. Instead, I built a wall of lies around me, and it is now that I am seeing this wall and what it has done to my soul. Finally facing this certainty—and the feelings of deep sadness, anger, and disappointment with myself—has shown me that the light is there. There is still hope for me to turn my life around. Acknowledging this today will make me better for tomorrow.

With love,

THE WORD FOREVER

Living in the present darkness
The word "forever" seems like a lifetime sentence of
Suffering
Emptiness
Regret.
Living in the present light
The word "forever" seems like a journey toward
Love
Hope
Adventure
And making memories that will last forever.

FOREVER

*"No winter lasts forever; no spring
skips its turn."* —Hal Borland

Grief takes the form of heartbreak. Even if the person is still living, the loss of a significant person has a profound effect. In the immediate aftermath of a breakup, you can still be reeling from the shock of the loss, setting off a stress response.[15] If we keep hanging onto memories that haunt us, we cannot fully live in the moment. Replaying and reliving moments in our past relationships will only create a vicious cycle of emotions that no longer serve us.

The word "forever" may feel like a lifetime sentence of suffering, but only if we choose to think that our heartbreak pain will have no end. When we choose to live with a painful experience for an extended period, it is difficult to feel a sense of hope. The heartbreak pain will subside, but only if we acknowledge it and allow ourselves to feel all the pain. So, take the time to grieve the loss of a loved one, whether it was your choice or not. If the loss is too painful to manage on your own, please seek professional help.

As much as many people want to quickly move on from a breakup, allowing time for yourself is crucial to the healing process. If closure is what you are seeking, do it! To fully move on from the past is to face it. Accept your part and speak your peace. If the necessary steps are not taken, that is when the word "forever" may seem like a lifetime sentence of suffering. Step into the light and make the word "forever" a once-in-lifetime journey toward something amazing.

LETTER #17

Dear Present,

I know you are worried about me. I am working on finding a way to clear my thoughts about Past. My thoughts are still lingering about making peace with Past. I don't understand why this is happening. I love my life with you. You fill my days with an abundance of joy, and I'm conscious of choosing you each day. It is time to silence those voices from Past so I can be at peace.

I can't give up now. This is where I am meant to be, and that is with you.

With love,

NEW DAY

Tranquility enters
A breath of a new day
A sigh of relief that yesterday is gone
Warmth emerges
And out pours
Hope for the impossible.

FINDING PEACE FROM WITHIN

"If you are depressed, you are living in the past. If you are anxious, you are living in the future. If you are at peace, you are living in the present." —Lao Tzu

When we feel down about a situation we regret, living fully in the present is difficult. We must know we have the power and total control to change our feelings. If we change our thoughts about a situation, we can change the course of our happiness. It is our negative thoughts that cause our pain and suffering. We must choose a positive interpretation of what is going on in our lives. The answers we need are found within.

Through meditation, journalling, and exercising, you can gain clarity and find what your soul is pursuing. The time has come to silence the negative voices, to finally shut them down. Peace is within your reach. Just grab it, and go!

Once you are at peace from within, you will attract more positivity into your life. New relationships will flourish, and you can be happy again. You have the choice of how you want to move forward.

LETTER #18

Dear Present,

I have been allowing my memories of Past to hold me back from truly being happy. This has been weighing me down. Since I couldn't seem to figure it out on my own, I turned to exploring my past lives for guidance, delving into multiple lifetimes in search of truth.

Following numerous visits to my past lives, the same emotions arose each time: the feelings of upset and frustration. After careful reflection, the feelings are parallel in this lifetime. These feelings are a mirror image of what I have been carrying inside me all these years. For things to be healed, just as my past life coach instructed, they have to be released. So, this is what I must do—release!

With love,

Regret

KARMA CLEANSE

Cleanse my soul
From all past regrets.
Help me send forth love and light to others.
Fill my heart with gratitude and a positive attitude.
Leave space to keep on forgiving.

KARMIC BOOMERANG

*"What goes around, comes around." —*Unknown

The Sanskrit word karma refers to the cycle of cause and effect, which states that every action a person performs in life will eventually have an impact on them. This guideline encompasses both a person's words and ideas.[16]

Karma comes down to the notion that our actions and words affect what will happen to us. No matter how we behave—whether we are honest or dishonest, whether we help or damage people—it all gets recorded. It will show up as a karmic consequence in this incarnation or others to come. The soul carries all of its karma with it into the next life.[17]

As humans, this may seem alarming because all of us have made choices at some point in our lives that were not in the best interest of others or ourselves, resulting in regret. This is where the karmic boomerang takes effect; what we do unto others will return to us. Therefore, we must learn how our actions can truly impact others and how we should show more compassion. You get what you give!

For those who believe in past lives, exploring past lives can help heal the present. According to past life coach Dr. Alishia M. Alibhai, we all have a soul that is within us and lives in lifetime after lifetime. When we pass on, we reincarnate into another body. We have the ability to tap into the wisdom of our soul. Our soul contains the knowledge within us. The things we have experienced in our past lives (relationships, struggles, how we died, health issues) can be impacting our lives today, without us even noticing. Exploring past lives can help us heal the present.[18]

There are two ways in which you can explore your past lives. One way is to retrieve information through guided meditations. Another way is to look for the clues around you in your present life. Notice if there is anything that stands out to you. These clues can be connected to a past life. Parallels or similar situations to your past lives might appear in dreams or your daily life. There is a wealth of information available about who you were in a past life.[19] With support from a past life coach can help you piece it together to empower you in this lifetime.

LETTER #19

Dear Present,

I am starting to understand what it took to get here with you. Looking back on my life, I see that what I did to Past brought me to you. It's everything in my history that shaped me into the person I am today. Of course, I would have liked to change some things, but it had to happen like this for whatever reason.

I have to remind myself that I was young and naive and did my best with what I believed to be true at that time. I did not want to hurt anyone, so I kept some of the truth to myself. Maybe by doing so, I was forced to be with you sooner as I knew you were the best for me. Each decision— good or bad—led me to you. But I could not have done it on my own. Past was a huge part of it, whether you like it or not. I can't erase Past, nor would I ever erase you.

With love,

Regret

REWIND

Rewind,
Nostalgia kicks in
Emotions stir
Senses heighten
I'm back to you.
Fast forward,
Gratitude steps up
Calmness takes over
It's me because of you.

THE BUTTERFLY EFFECT

"You have been created in order to make a difference. You have within you the power to change the world." —Andy Andrews

The phrase "butterfly effect" was coined by a meteorologist named Edward Lorenz in the 1960s. It came after he realized that small adjustments to the initial conditions of his computer weather models could cause anything from sunny skies to violent storms, with no way to foresee the outcome.[20]

In the present, we can look back on the past and analyze how events and people came to be in our lives, whether for a short or extended period, and their placement on our timeline. The butterfly effect explains how unimportant factors can have a nonlinear effect on complex systems.[21] We must look back and see the bigger picture, our present life. Small events can serve as catalysts that will take effect over time and change our lives considerably.

By looking back on the minute details of our lives, we can see more vividly that all the small events and decisions we have made led us to who we are meant to be today. As chaotic as it may have felt, the chaos created the order in our lives.

LETTER #20

Dear Present,

Something is captivating about the moon. As I look up at the luminous full moon, I can't help but think about my past, present, and future. It's Past that made me who I am today, you, Present, who keeps me grounded, and prospects of the future that make me hopeful. I'm pulled into the night sky as if it's sending me messages, and I'm receiving them just as the moon receives light from the sun.

Thanks to you, I'm trying to be like the moon. The moon is a beacon of light in the night and guides us in the darkness. I'm trying to be that light to others by living in the present and sharing my love of life. There was a time so long ago when I thought the light was out inside, but then you came along and lit it up.

Thank you for being my light and guiding me into a bright future!

With love,

LOOKING UP AT OUR MOON

The phases repeat
From days
To
Weeks
To
Months
To
Years.
Waiting patiently
For the perfect time to
Appear.
Faith kept me company,
Hope kept me going,
And
Love kept me strong.
Looking up at our moon
Is how I held on.

TALKING TO THE MOON

*"And like the moon, we must go through phases of emptiness to feel whole again." —*Unknown

Looking up at the night sky makes the world seem so enchanting. As vast and complex as the world may appear, we are all somehow intertwined. The energy is there, flowing through and around us. Seeing the moon in all its beauty and knowing that we all share the same moon can only confirm that we can still look up at it and speak to one another. It is the same moon in the past and the present, and it will be the same moon in the future.

Moon signs in astrology stand for a deep, soulful aspect of who we are that we cannot explain in words. The moon talks to our sense of comfort and our recollections or concepts of the past.[22] Additionally, this planetary alignment can reveal to you what drives you from the depths of your subconscious mind as well as your specific desires for this lifetime. Your moon sign helps you better grasp the emotional foundation of who you are, what you feel, and why you feel the way you do.[23]

This can provide valuable insight for many individuals who are striving to understand themselves on an emotional level. Taking a deeper look into the version of ourselves that we keep hidden from others can help us better understand our subconscious and how we relate to our emotions.

Sometimes the deep emotions we keep hidden need to be visible, just as the moon becomes visible at night.

According to my moon sign, the moon in Scorpio means there is a need to delve into your feelings as deeply as possible. This is exactly what I am finally doing at this stage in my life. I find it interesting that this moon sign states that my emotions run deep. This sign shares their buried truths with only a few chosen souls, and they tend to desire deep personal connections. This speaks true to me. As outgoing as I may seem, there is more to me than meets the eye, and only a few people truly know the other side.

The moon goes through phases, and so do we. Sometimes we show people all we are; other times, we keep part of ourselves hidden and maybe show nothing. Each phase we go through brings upon change. With the change, we must let go of what no longer serves us or aligns with our path.

One way to help guide you in changing is participating in a full moon meditation. There are different themes for each full moon depending on the position of the planets. During a full moon, you can use the moon's power to let go of any regrets, reflect on your past or current living situation, and manifest something extraordinary into your life.

LETTER #21

Dear Present,

I'm starting to see miracles right before my eyes because of you. My life without Past is starting to feel permanent. I feel stronger and happier, and I genuinely want to be with you. It just took me a while to figure it out.

It's a miracle that we found each other. Rarely does one's soul recognize where it should be. I'm starting to realize that my life with Past is over, and my decisions led me on this path to you.

Thank you for being patient with me and believing our love will stand the test of time.

With love,

MY SIGNS

It's a miracle that my signs have come
To reassure
To confirm
To proclaim
That what I am seeking
Is coming
True.

MIRACLES

"There are only two ways to live your life. One is as though nothing is a miracle. The other is as though everything is a miracle." —Albert Einstein

Miracles can be found every day. We need to be open to the idea that blessings can come to us and from us. Once we quiet our minds, we can hear God calling. When we receive messages and signs, that is a miracle! As much as we want to believe from the inside, we must put forth work from the outside. For faith to exist, you have to take action. And with action comes patience. Waiting is the hardest thing, but the most important, regarding miracles. As with anything good in life, it is worth the wait. Waking up to a new day is a miracle! It is a fresh start to get you going and welcome you to the present. Sometimes that is all we need—to recognize that life is the miracle we are blessed with, and we must cherish it and be grateful.

LETTER #22

Dear Present,

Focusing on living in this moment gives me perspective on the lessons I have learned to help me carry on. I know I didn't do the right thing back then, but I promised myself from the moment you came into my life that I would always be honest and loyal to you.

This is my "ah ha" moment, that at the end of the day, all that matters is that I have the power to accept and forgive myself to move on. As hard as this lesson has been, I could not have learned it earlier as I was not ready to let go and move forward. But here I am now; the time has come, and my heart is finally at peace. There are no more tears left to cry, and although there are scars on my heart, they no longer hurt. I needed to be with you to realize this truth.

From this day on, I will honour and cherish each day together!

With love,

Regret

FREE FROM THE PAST

At last,
I am free
From the past.
A time that no longer exists.
The teacher served the period.
The lessons have been taught.
I am here today with forgiveness
That only I can hold,
And a future that is waiting to be told.

FORGIVENESS

"Forgive yourself for not knowing what you didn't know before you learned it." —Maya Angelou

Forgiveness can be the most challenging thing to achieve, but it is something we must all embrace at some point in our lives. We owe it to our future. For some people, the intense feelings of guilt and shame can take away years of not living in the present. Forgiving others and ourselves leads to a more satisfying life, physically, emotionally, mentally, and spiritually. To forgive, we must be intentional and allow ourselves to let go of our anger, resentment, and deep regret. By seeking forgiveness or by forgiving, we can move forward and live a life showing compassion, empathy, and respect for others and ourselves.

Learning how to forgive yourself is a choice. By forgiving yourself, you are finally accepting what has happened and are ready to move forward. Consider these approaches for granting yourself forgiveness by psychology educator Kendra Cherry:

1. Understand your emotions.
2. Accept responsibility for what happened.
3. Treat yourself with kindness and compassion.
4. Express remorse for your mistakes.
5. Make amends and apologize (including apologizing to yourself).

6. Look for ways to learn from the experience.
7. Focus on making better choices in the future.[24]

During this stage of forgiveness, you can at last release the burden of guilt that has been holding you back. This would be a good opportunity for you to write yourself an apology letter. Take the time to reflect inward and write out the words you need to set yourself free. Focus on all the emotions that you keep inside and explore why they are there. What did you learn from your mistakes? How is your remorse going to lead you? And, finally, give yourself some encouraging and uplifting words to inspire you to make a change for the better.

American fiction writer, Ted Chiang states it best in his fantasy novelette, *The Merchant and the Alchemist's Gate*, "Nothing erases the past. There is repentance, there is atonement, and there is forgiveness. That is all, but that is enough."[25]

PART III:
THE FUTURE

115

THE ROAD TO THE
GREAT UNKNOWN

SINCE THE FUTURE is unwritten, Regret does not exist, and, subsequently, there are no letters in this section. Each topic will address what you can do today to help your future self. May your journey to the great unknown provide you with insight and steer you in the right direction, to living a life you genuinely love and deserve.

23. THE FUTURE IS WAITING

"The best way to predict the future is to create it." —Abraham Lincoln

The future is waiting for you. It is a time that has not yet arrived. Research suggests that thinking about the future—a process known as prospection—can help people lead more generous and fulfilled lives.[26] For some people, thinking about the future may cause stress and anxiety, but for others, it is something to look forward to. Thinking about what the future may hold allows you to think of the possibilities you can choose from in the now.

What we do in the present can help limit our regrets in the future. The regrets of the past can be used to help gain clarity on what you value. If you spend time carefully making decisions while considering the impact of regret, this will influence the kind of outcome you hope to obtain in the future.

Here are some recommendations you can do today to limit future regrets:

- Think before you speak and do.

- Let go of fear.
- Be aware that for every action or inaction, there will be an impact on yourself and/or others.
- Recognize what you want in life.
- Think about what your future self would do.
- Follow your dreams!
- Be open to change.
- Take care of your mental, spiritual, and physical health.
- Accept others for who they are.
- Value time.

24. CHASE YOUR FUTURE SELF

"Twenty years from now you will be more disappointed by the things that you didn't do than by the ones you did do, so throw off the bowlines, sail away from the safe harbor, catch the trade winds in your sails. Explore. Dream. Discover." —Mark Twain

Matthew McConaughey conveyed it brilliantly when he won Best Actor at the eighty-sixth Academy Awards in 2014: he said his hero was his future self. His hero to chase was him in ten years; and when those ten years came to pass, it would be him again in the years ahead. He stated he would never become his hero or even attain heroism, and he was okay with that because he would always have somebody to keep on chasing.[27] As we should with ourselves. We are never done because we are always changing and have room to keep growing and getting better with time.

The future is unrecorded, and we are unsure what the future will hold and who we will become. If you could give your younger self advice, what would it be?

If I could speak to my younger self, I would say:

- Dream BIG!
- Take more risks.
- Always strive for the best.
- Be a leader, not a follower.
- Don't be too hard on yourself.
- Don't give your heart away too easily.
- Don't judge others; get to know people's stories.
- Your reputation follows you, so treat others as you want to be treated.
- You can't rely on others to make you happy—only you can find happiness from within.

It is what we do today that will impact our future selves. Let us strive to become the best versions of ourselves, so that one day we can look back and be proud of our journey.

25. THE VEHICLE WE DRIVE

"There are far, far better things ahead than any we leave behind." —C.S. Lewis

A remarkably close friend of mine shared a homily from her priest on New Year's Day 2023. She mentioned the analogy was a perfect message for me about the future. It went something like this: You take a vehicle to get to where you must go in life. In the vehicle, you have to look out the wide window in front of you, and only once in a while do you need to look back by using the rearview mirrors. The same is true in life— you need to look ahead to get to the future, and only once in a while should you look back at what you left behind, when it serves you.

If we see our souls as the vehicles we drive, we need to start taking better care of ourselves, so we can last a long time.

Here are a few ways to care for our souls:

- Watch out for the signs—they show up time and time again in mysterious ways.
- Look around at your surroundings and the people you allow to occupy your space.

- Drive with caution.
- Act with prudence and don't let your emotions control your behaviour.
- Take your time and don't rush into things—life is not a speedway to race; it's a journey to enjoy.
- If you get hurt, take the necessary time to care for and heal yourself.

26. BE THE CHANGE

"Be the change you wish to see in the world." —Mahatma Gandhi

Each day we are given a chance to make a positive change within ourselves, leading us to put good into the world. It is a conscious decision that must occur in our minds, be felt in our hearts, and put forth in our actions. This inner transformation requires us to reflect honestly on ourselves and show no judgment as we learn from our past regrets.

Life is like a journey on a winding road, with unexpected twists and turns. Your journey toward your purpose in life will not be easy. You need to prepare yourself for the ups and downs. Cruise the opportunities when they come along and if you get off track, may you find your way back. It is how you respond to your life's situations that will dictate the outcome of your future.

Here are several actions you can take to enhance your happiness:

- Practice gratitude every day. Each night before you go to sleep, go through all the blessings of your day.

- Focus on the good, no matter what is happening in your life.
- Laugh—laughter is truly the best medicine, even when the laughter is at your expense.
- Smile—smiling from the outside creates a smile on the inside. And the more you smile, the more others will smile back. Try it! It is contagious.
- Surround yourself with a positive group of people. Like-minded, positive people bring out the best in each other.
- Engage in positive self-talk, especially when your thoughts start to get negative. As soon as that negative thought sets in and wants to take over, you must immediately insert a new thought that is positive and uplifting. You are what you think, so think the best!
- Teach what you preach—try your hardest to live a life full of good values and morals.

There are moments when we need to temporarily allow ourselves to feel the negative emotions, but do not dwell and live in them too long. The key to happiness is finding the good from within and sharing it with others. We have the power to train our brains to think more positively, and through our actions, we can be the change in this world.

27. THE POWER OF WORDS

"Kind words can be short and easy to speak, but their echoes are truly endless." —St. Teresa of Calcutta

For things to be healed, you must release them. Do not be haunted by words left unspoken. Those healing words must come out of you to free yourself from the past. Those words may not have come out then, but they can now. Our words are so powerful, and they hold the energy to heal. We can speak to the past, present, and future with our words. Through the energy of our words, we can speak with clarity and certainty to the universe to help create new circumstances. Use the power of your words to speak your truth, put forth good energy, and help make peace with others. Use your words to make a positive change, and those changes will impact your future.

Before you speak, ask yourself:

- Will my words hurt or heal?
- Is what I'm about to say true?
- What are the intentions behind my words?
- Will I regret what I'm about to say?

- What good will come out of what I'm about to say?
- How will my words impact the person I'm talking to?
- What emotions are underlying my words?
- Are the words coming from my heart or someone else's?

28. MOVING FORWARD

"Life can only be understood backwards, but it must be lived forwards." —Søren Kierkegaard

Moving forward means that we have to leave something behind. Looking back at what we left behind—which no longer served us—can teach us some valuable lessons. When we look back at what we did not say or should have said, we can learn and commit to not repeating the same mistakes. It reveals that we must be bold and speak up, especially when amends need to be made. Looking back helps us make better choices in the future.

Regret researcher and author, Daniel H. Pink writes in his book, *The Power of Regret: How Looking Backward Moves Us Forward*, "Looking backward can move us forward, but only if we do it right. The sequence of self-disclosure, self-compassion, and self-distancing offers a simple yet systematic way to transform regret into a powerful force for stability, achievement, and purpose."[28] There are many great benefits to be had, both physically and mentally, when we speak our truth or write it out. The most crucial aspect of dealing with all forms of regret is disclosing it.

The next step is to address our regrets with self-compassion. We need to allow ourselves to steer away from judgment and instead show ourselves some kindness. Pink states, "The people who addressed their regret with self-compassion were more likely to change their behavior than those who approached their regret with self-esteem."[29]

The last step is self-distancing. It is best to examine your regret as a neutral observer rather than as yourself. Next, imagine visiting the future and examining the regret retrospectively. Lastly, shift your language; use third-person pronouns instead of referring to yourself as "I," "me," or "my." How we view ourselves helps us gain a clearer perspective on regrets.[30]

If we take the time to look backward to help us move forward, taking control of what we can and letting go of what we cannot, we have the power to create our redemption and finally set ourselves free.[31]

Moving forward into the future, regret can teach you to do the following:

- Listen to your intuition
- Follow your heart
- Speak your truth
- Find the courage to move forward
- Be wise and learn from your mistakes

29. WHAT NEXT?

"Intuition will tell the thinking mind
what to do next." —Jonas Salk

At the end of the day, ask yourself: Did I do the best I possibly could to the best of my abilities? If you answered yes, you should be satisfied. If you answered no, what can you change today for a better tomorrow? Life is not set; it involves ongoing changes, and what you change will affect your future.

It is never too late to change; age is never a factor. If you have the courage, you can do anything your heart desires.

According to author, Vex King, "Your circumstances don't define your destiny, but your response to them does. Meet pain with positivity, hate with kindness, and fear with faith. Pray for those who wish to see you suffer. You can only control the energy you put out there—and this determines your future."[32]

Here are some steps you can take to help you move forward:

- Don't let other people's opinions influence your thoughts and beliefs—they don't know your inner self, so listen to the call inside.
- Stop putting off what you can do today to tomorrow—seize the day!
- Commit to changing, and you will change!
- Discover your purpose—what is your why in life?

30. FAITH OVER FEAR

"Faith and fear both demand you believe in something you cannot see. You choose." —Bob Proctor

The Bible says in Hebrew 11:1 that only faith can guarantee the blessings that we hope for or prove the existence of realities that are unseen.

The concept of faith is difficult for many people to comprehend or believe in. To believe in the unknown or unseen requires faith, which begins in our hearts and shows itself through our actions.

Fear is the complete absence of faith. Fear is a normal and natural response to demanding situations, but how we respond to our fears makes all the difference. We have a choice: let fear control us and run our lives OR face our fears and trust that God will help and save us.

To overcome fear, we must understand why and how it got there. If we do not, fear can consume our every thought. We do not want to project our past mistakes into our future and take away from us the hope for a better tomorrow. This is why we need to choose faith over fear!

We cannot let fear drive us. If we do, it will lead us to darkness and a life unfulfilled. Some people believe we have this one life to live, so we must live it and make it count by embracing abundant goodness. Remember, you are the driver in this life, and you have control over what will steer it. Will it be faith or fear?

Faith over fear welcomes peace, happiness, and courage to help us move forward despite uncertainty. Faith over fear is a lifelong journey, and we must be patient. Whatever your belief is, allow it to guide you out of the darkness and into the light. If you do this, regret will not be present.

31. HOPE

"Hope is the last thing ever lost." —Italian proverb

Hope is not of the past, but a positive mindset of the possibilities that can come to light in the future. Researcher Chan Hellman states in his article, "The Science and Power of Hope and How to Nurture it in Youth and Adults," hope is defined as "the belief that our future can be better than our past and that we have a role to play in making that future a reality."[33]

The word hope is immensely powerful. To have hope, one must want a specific outcome that will make their life better. Through the power of hope, we can get through what seems like an unbearable situation and know that it is temporary. Having hope can ultimately improve our lives, by visualizing the steps to a better future. With hope, we can reduce our stress and feelings of helplessness and improve our quality of life. So, choose hope. "Let your hopes, not your hurts, shape your future."[34]

As I was drafting this book, my daughter came home with her Grade 9 religion textbook and was working on some questions for her last unit of study called, "Be Hopeful." I informed her that it was very fitting with what I was writing about. I took her book and read through the first topic lesson, and I was inspired by the many ways hope can be viewed.

Here is my version of what hope can provide for us:

- Hope empowers us to be brave and share ourselves with others.
- Hope offers us a chance to be vulnerable.
- Hope motivates us to keep moving forward.
- Hope unlocks our heart's desires.
- Hope heals our pain from the past.
- Hope empowers us to make necessary changes.
- Hope supports our dreams and aspirations.
- Hope influences us to find the good in others.
- Hope harbours us when we feel lost.
- Hope shields us from darkness and helplessness.

32. THE HEALING POWER OF LOVE

"We look forward to the time when the Power of Love will replace the Love of Power. Then will our world know the blessings of peace." —William E. Gladstone

You must reconnect to the pure love within you to heal your life and experience a promising future. It is through this reconnection that you will return to being whole. The love within us can bring the body and soul back into balance. "Love is a healing agent because its energetic frequency is stronger than other emotions and is the foundation of universal order."[35]

The famous saying, "You need to learn to love yourself before you can love others," is true. But why is it so hard, even though the outcome will lead to a more fulfilled life? Love is the key to unlocking a transformative life filled with self-worth, stronger relationships, and better decision-making. Loving yourself first will result in fewer regrets.

Author and motivational speaker, Mel Robbins shared in one of her podcasts, that "being kinder to yourself and learning how to accept and love yourself is the biggest mover in terms of your happiness."[36]

Here are a few ways to help you learn how to love yourself more:

- Recognize the good in yourself.
- Get in tune with the energy of your heart.
- Engage in positive self-talk.
- Create and maintain a self-care routine.
- Make time to partake in activities you enjoy.

The most powerful and purest form of love is agape, which is unconditional love. In 1 Corinthians 13, the Bible describes love as patient, kind, compassionate, forbearing, forgiving, honourable, and unselfish. These are all the attributes that describe God. When we tap into our deepest authentic selves, we, too, are agape.

Here are some of the best ways to cultivate more love according to functional medicine consultant Dr. Jill Carnahan:

- Stay connected with others, especially real-life connections.
- Tell others how you feel.
- Be generous.
- Release the "love hormones" with physical touch.
- Meditate and pray.
- Eat well.[37]

Take the time now to love yourself, and have love renew and restore your inner harmony. Your future depends on it!

33. TAKE THE ROAD LESS TRAVELLED

"Two roads diverged in a wood, and I,
I took the one less traveled by,
And that has made all the difference." —Robert Frost

In life, we can do what was stated in Robert Frost's poem "The Road Not Taken" and take the road less travelled. We need to follow our own paths. Some of us live a life of indecision and allow the fear of making the wrong decision to paralyze us, creating a lifetime of pain, regret, and despair. How do we want to look back on our choices? Do we want to look back with regret or gratitude?

The choices we make, whether they are big or small, impact our future selves. Each decision sets us on a path we may not understand in the present, but may understand later in the future. After that, we can look back and see the moments that led to where we are destined to be. In retrospect, we can understand which choices made the biggest difference and had the most significant impact. Looking back on the past can give certainty and wisdom in understanding our path in life.

When we come to a crossroads, we must take the time to reflect and analyze our choices and commit to following one wherever it may lead. We must accept it and move forward, as the other path will no longer exist. Take your time: Choose wisely and remember to enjoy the journey!

MY WISH FOR YOU

TODAY IS YOUR day to start and pave a new future. This is the time to act and put the work in to end your suffering. No more letting regret continue to weigh heavy in your heart. Use your time wisely, reflect on your life, and determine what you need to do to make peace with your past mistakes.

As much as many of us wish we could go back in time to change history, we cannot, but what we can do is make changes today! Take hold of the time you have and speak your truth, however hard it may be. Start making a list of all those people from your past you want to make amends with. If it is possible, try to reach out. Speaking your truth not only feels good but may also offer healing and closure to both parties involved.

To my readers, my wish for you is the same wish I have for myself and my loved ones . . . to live a life you genuinely love. Whether you believe in one life or many, it all comes down to the same thing: Make your life count! Go out and make a positive difference in this world. It all starts and ends with you.

May your road to the great unknown be filled with adventure, understandable signs, smooth highways, many green lights, and easy navigation. If you get lost or come across bumpy roads, detours, or stop signs, take time to brake, then keep going. Find your way to your destination, and look back with a full heart with no regrets!

ACKNOWLEDGMENTS

WORDS CANNOT TRULY express my deepest gratitude to the countless people who supported me through this journey of writing my first book. I am so grateful and blessed to have my family, relatives, friends, colleagues, and FriesenPress Publishing to cheer me on every step of the way.

I am eternally grateful to my loving and supportive family. Thank you to my husband, Rob, and daughters Giulia and Vanessa for encouraging me to take the time to pursue my calling to write this book. I deeply appreciate you all listening to me share my ideas and read my chapters out repeatedly, and I am grateful you allowed me to teach you all to speak your truth. Rob, thank you for reading my manuscript, sharing your excitement, and believing I could dig even deeper. And thank you to my sweet dog, Auston, who was by my side every day for a year while I was writing this book.

To my parents, Frances and Clyde Hiscock: Thank you for your unconditional love and always wanting the best for me. How you both raised me instilled the goodness in me that I share with others.

To my nana Maria Bitonti, although you are not here with me physically, I can feel your presence every day. You filled my heart with your strength and insight. Thank you for sharing your words of wisdom and being my compass in life. Hearing your regrets pushed me to write this book. I hope you left this world at peace with your past.

To the first readers of my manuscript: my aunt Audrey Stringer, my brother Charles Hiscock, and my friends Carla Shafer and Anna Spadafora Kalika. Whether you read the manuscript in its entirety or just partially, thank you for taking the time to read it, share your feedback, and push me to open up more.

To my relatives and in-laws near and far—the Hiscocks, Buonomos, Oliverios, Logullos, and Bitontis (that's including all my aunts, uncles, cousins, mother-in-law and father-in-law, brothers-in-law and sisters-in-law, nieces, nephews, and their significant others): Thank you all for sharing your anticipation with me and checking in to see how I was progressing. A special thanks to my sister-in-law Nadia Oliverio. Your enthusiasm for my journey was truly uplifting.

A heartfelt thank you to my cousins Lucy Belcastro and Sue Thorpe, and long-time childhood friend Maria Gentile Hillier: Thank you for taking the time to meet with me often or just call frequently to discuss my manuscript. You all have a special place in my heart as we all share similar views about life. Also, to my cousin Ida-Marie Logullo: Thank you for sharing your knowledge of Islam's view of destiny.

To all my colleagues that are truly my friends, especially Amanda Resch and Adriana Burton: Your time and listening ears, especially during my year off, meant so much to me.

To Stephanie Hrehirchuk, who came into my life because of my aunt Barb Bitonti. Thank you for meeting up with me, listening to the beginning ideas of my book, and working with me to go over the first draft of my manuscript. Your kindness and words of wisdom truly gave me the push to see this dream out.

To my amazing and talented friend Joanne Bryant. Thank you for spending the time going over my earliest manuscript draft and taking on the role of the artist to create the most beautiful piece of artwork for my book cover. Your work is truly inspirational, and I feel so blessed to showcase your talent on my cover.

To my talented nephew Joseph Oliverio: Thank you for capturing my author's headshot on a smoky day and turning the pictures into a work of art.

To the outstanding FriesenPress team: Thank you for all your hard work and support from day one, especially Christoph Koniczek, publishing consultant, for answering all my questions and welcoming me to the company. To my publishing specialist, Lee-Ann Jaworski, and team: Thank you for keeping me on track and guiding me in managing every detail of my book while it went through the publishing process. Leïta, my editor, thank you for all your time and hard work making sure my work was at its best. And thank you to the cover designer who took the beautiful artwork, created an eye-catching cover title, and made my vision a reality.

Thank you to God for giving me this precious life to live to the fullest and having the Holy Spirit guide me to write out all the words that have been left unspoken.

Finally, to the readers for picking up this book and supporting my dream of making a difference in the lives of many. May this message speak to you and spread amongst the people you know and love.

ENDNOTES

1   Brown, Brené. *Atlas of the Heart: Mapping Meaningful Connection and the Language of Human Experience.* Random House Publishing Group, 2021.

2   Heshmat, Shahram. "Why Does Music Evoke Memories?" *Psychology Today*, 14 September 2021, www.psychologytoday.com/ca/blog/science-choice/202109/why-does-music-evoke-memories. Accessed 29 April 2023.

3   Victor, David. "Music as a Universal Language of Healing." *Harmony & Healing*, 3 April 2023, www.harmonyandhealing.org/music-as-a-universal-language-of-healing/#:~:text=The%20sound%20and%20rhythm%20of,the%20essence%20of%20Harmony%20%26%20Healing! Accessed 29 April 2023.

4   BITESIZE. "Life after death - Judgement - Key beliefs in Judaism - GCSE Religious Studies Revision - AQA." *BBC*, www.bbc.co.uk/bitesize/guides/zh9vgdm/revision/2. Accessed 17 October 2023.

5   Ukachi, Austen C. "Destiny 2: The Christian View About Destiny | The Guardian Nigeria News - Nigeria

and World News — Sunday Magazine — The Guardian Nigeria News – Nigeria and World News." *The Guardian Nigeria*, 1 October 2017, guardian.ng/sunday-magazine/ibru-ecumenical-centre/destiny-2-the-christian-view-about-destiny/. Accessed 28 September 2023.

6   Vorng, Sophorntavy. "Fate (Buddhism)." *Encyclopedia of Scientific Dating Methods*, 2017, pp. 485–487, link.springer.com/referenceworkentry/10.10 07%2F978-94-024-0852-2_212, https://doi.org/10.1007/978-94-024-0852-2_212. Accessed 6 December 2021.

7   Yahya, Harun. "True Muslims Believe in Destiny." *Arab News*, 11 June 2015, www.arabnews.com/islam-per-spective/news/760546. Accessed 28 September 2023.

8   Chiu, Allyson. "Do Dreams Mean Anything? Why Do I Feel Like I'm Falling? Or Wake up Paralyzed? We Asked Experts." *The Washington Post*, 30 December 2021, www.washingtonpost.com/wellness/2021/12/30/do-dreams-have-meaning/. Accessed 29 April 2023.

9   Alibhai, Alishia M. "Exploring Past Lives: A Journey into the Hidden Realm of the Soul." Course pack, compiled by Dr. Alishia Alibhai, 2021, www.divinebliss.ca.

10 Winfrey, Oprah. *The Wisdom of Sundays: Life-Changing Insights from Super Soul Conversations*. Flatiron Books, 2017.

11 Wong, Kenneth. "How to Set an Intention for Manifestation in 3 Steps." *The Millennial Grind*, 29 April 2021, millennial-grind.com/how-to-set-an-intention-for-manifestation-in-3-steps/. Accessed 29 April 2023.

12 Bernstein, Gabrielle. *The Universe Has Your Back: Transform Fear to Faith*. Hay House, 2016.

13 Pueblo, Yung. "Ego, Pain, and Attachment." *Elevate with Yung Pueblo*, 6 Apr. 2021, yungpueblo.substack.com/p/ego-pain-and-attachment. Accessed 29 April 2023.

14 Babour, Hugh. "The Secret Reason the Devil Tempts Us." *Catholic Answers*, 21 February 2021, www.catholic.com/magazine/online-edition/the-secret-reason-the-devil-tempts-us. Accessed 3 October 2023.

15 Bryars, Ziella. "How to Ease the Pain of Heartache." *Psyche*, 28 July 2021, psyche.co/guides/how-to-ease-the-pain-of-grief-following-a-romantic-breakup. Accessed 3 October 2023.

16 Strada, Dina. *5 Steps to Karmic Cleansing and Erasing Karmic Debt*, chopra.com/articles/5-steps-to-give-yourself-a-karmic-cleanse. Accessed 29 April 2023.

17 Dasa, Pandit. "Karma: What Goes Around Comes Around." *HuffPost*, 11 November 2011, www.huffpost.com/entry/karma-what-goes-around-comes-around_b_1081057. Accessed 29 April 2023.

18 Alibhai, Alishia M. "Exploring Past Lives: A Journey into the Hidden Realm of the Soul." Course pack, compiled by Dr. Alishia Alibhai, 2021, www.divinebliss.ca.

19 Alibhai, Alishia M. "Exploring Past Lives: A Journey into the Hidden Realm of the Soul." Course pack, compiled by Dr. Alishia Alibhai, 2021, www.divinebliss.ca.

20 APS News. *Butterflies, Tornadoes, and Time Travel*. vol. 13, www.aps.org/publications/apsnews/200406/butterfly-effect.cfm. Accessed 29 April 2023.

21 Farman Street. "The Butterfly Effect: Everything You Need to Know About This Powerful Mental Model." fs.blog/the-butterfly-effect/. Accessed 29 April 2023.

22 Stardust, Lisa. "Sun, Moon and Rising Sign Meaning: What to Know About Astrological Big Three." *TODAY*, 6 May 2022, www.today.com/life/astrology/sun-moon-rising-meaning-rcna23286. Accessed 5 June 2023.

23 Rose, Meghan. "What Is My Moon Sign? How to Find Yours—And What It Means." *Glamour*, 31 May 2022, www.glamour.com/story/what-is-my-moon-sign. Accessed 5 June 2023.

24 Cherry, Kendra. "How to Forgive Yourself: Tips for Self-Forgiveness." *Verywell Mind*, 20 February 2023, www.verywellmind.com/how-to-forgive-yourself-4583819. Accessed 17 October 2023.

25 Chiang, Ted. *The Merchant and the Alchemist's Gate.* Subterranean Press, 2007.

26 Allen, Summer. "How Thinking About the Future Makes Life More Meaningful." *Greater Good Science Center*, 1 May 2019, greatergood.berkeley.edu/article/item/how_thinking_about_the_future_makes_life_more_meaningful. Accessed 29 April 2023.

27 "Matthew McConaughey Winning Best Actor." *YouTube*, 11 Mar. 2014, www.youtube.com/watch?v=wD2cVhC-63I. Accessed 28 September 2023.

28 Pink, Daniel H. *The Power of Regret: How Looking Backward Moves Us Forward.* Penguin Publishing Group, 2022.

29 Pink, Daniel H. *The Power of Regret: How Looking Backward Moves Us Forward.* Penguin Publishing Group, 2022.

30 Pink, Daniel H. *The Power of Regret: How Looking Backward Moves Us Forward*. Penguin Publishing Group, 2022.

31 Pink, Daniel H. *The Power of Regret: How Looking Backward Moves Us Forward*. Penguin Publishing Group, 2022.

32 King, Vex. *Good Vibes, Good Life: How Self-Love Is the Key to Unlocking Your Greatness*. Hay House UK, 2018.

33 Hellman, Chan, and Casey Gwinn. "The Science and Power of Hope and How to Nurture it in Youth and Adults." *Prevention Technology Transfer Center (PTTC) Network*, 21 April 2021, pttcnetwork.org/centers/south-southwest-pttc/news/science-and-power-hope-and-how-nurture-it-youth-and-adults. Accessed 28 September 2023.

34 "Robert H. Schuller Quotes." *BrainyQuote.com*, 9 March 2019, www.brainyquote.com/citation/quotes/robert_h_schuller_156006. Accessed 9 October 2023.

35 Fahkry, Tony. "This Is Why The Power Of Love Will Heal Your Life." *Medium*, 9 October 2017, medium.com/the-mission/this-is-why-the-power-of-love-will-heal-your-life-f649b037ce78. Accessed 29 April 2023.

36 Robbins, Mel, host. "How Do I Learn to Love Myself, Really?" Mel Robbins Podcast. 27 Nov. 2022, www.youtube.com/watch?v=Wb9oN1720ws&t=3s. Accessed 5 March 2024.

37 Carnahan, Jill C. "Love Heals: The Powerful Effects of Love (and How To Create More of It)." *Dr. Jill Carnahan*, 11 February 2020, www.jillcarnahan.com/2020/02/11/love-heals/. Accessed 29 April 2023.

ABOUT THE AUTHOR

 BORN AND RAISED in Calgary, Alberta, Anna Marie Buonomo brings two decades of teaching experience to her role as an author. Regarded as a trusted confidant by many, Anna has heard countless tales of regret. Those stories, along with her own regrets, were the catalysts for this book. Her hope is that the challenges expressed within these pages, as well as the many words of encouragement that accompany them, will help people move away from self-limiting thoughts and toward a healthier and happier future.

In addition to helping others, Anna is passionate about reading, photography, and mental health. She holds a special place in her heart for moments spent with family and friends, especially with her husband Rob, and their teenage daughters Giulia and Vanessa. Together, they enjoy travelling and spending time with their sweet shorkie, Auston.

Printed in the USA
CPSIA information can be obtained
at www.ICGtesting.com
JSHW070214060724
65870JS00006B/12